VGM'S
CAREER
PORTRAITS

ACTING

ACTING

Jaq Greenspon

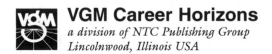

VGM Career Horizons
a division of NTC Publishing Group
Lincolnwood, Illinois USA

Photo Credits:
Page 43: Photo Network, Tustin, CA.
Pages 1, 15, 29, 57, and 71: Jeff Ellis Photography, Chicago.
All other photographs courtesy of the author.

Library of Congress Cataloging-in-Publication Data

Greenspon, Jaq.
    VGM's career portraits : acting / Jaq Greenspon.
      p.   cm.
    Includes index.
    Summary: Introduces such careers in the performing arts as
actor, singer, comedienne, and writer, using portraits of various
people in the field.
ISBN 0-8442-4379-5
    1. Theater—Vocational guidance—Juvenile literature.
[1. Performing arts—Vocational guidance. 2. Entertainers.
3. Vocational guidance.] I. Title.
PN2074.G74 1996   95-50610
792'.02'93—dc20   CIP
                                 AC

Published by VGM Career Horizons, a division of NTC Publishing Group
4255 West Touhy Avenue
Lincolnwood (Chicago), Illinois 60646-1975, U.S.A.

6 7 8 9 0 QB 9 8 7 6 5 4 3 2 1

Contents

Everybody's a hero
everybody's a star
everybody's in show biz
no matter who you are

The Kinks

Dedication

For Troy and Aren
Thanks for it all—again and again.

Introduction

Acting has been with us longer than the written word. When the caveman hunter Og told the other tribesmen about fighting a lion, that was a story. But when Og's friend Gog put the lion skin on and attacked Og in demonstration and Og used a piece of wood for the spear that killed the lion, then acting was born. Og and his friends were the first performers, and what they began has been passed along to us in the form of drama.

Since that time, drama has evolved quite a bit. Now, instead of just one person performing only one type of performance, there is a choice. Inside this book, you'll be presented with all of the different possibilities that will put you in the spotlight. Of course, if you don't want to perform, you'll also find out how to *operate* the spotlight!

Theatre is one of the most collaborative arts. One person alone can't do it. But a group of people, working together, can create something that lasts forever. But be warned: anyone can work in theatre, but once you start, it's very hard to stop!

Acknowledgments

Thanks to Tamara, for showing me anything is possible, to Matthew (and the entire Agoura High School Drama Department) for reminding me how fun theatre is, to the past, present, and future members of The Rainbow Co. Children's Theatre (Las Vegas, NV), for starting me out.

CAREERS IN DRAMA

The lights are low. As you step on stage a single light illuminates where you stand. A hush falls over the audience as you begin your soliloquy. You are contemplating life and its merits, summing up your thoughts. The audience is riveted as you go through a range of emotions, from joyous laughter to tears running down your face. As you finish and the lights dim, signifying the end of the play, you hear the applause and see the audience start to rise. You bow with pride.

1

What's it like to be a dramatic actor?

Spencer Tracy once said there are two things to being an actor: "Hit your mark and don't bump into the furniture." He was right, but he was also wrong. The first thing you have to know is your lines. In theatre, the words are very important. When you get your script, your first job is to study it and memorize your lines. While you are learning lines, you are also learning blocking. Blocking is your movement on the stage, where you are supposed to be when you say a line. Finally, you work with the director to get the emotion right. If the scene is about a birthday party and you are sad, it means something different than if you are happy.

Where do dramatic actors perform?

It's a myth that in order to be successful you have to perform on Broadway. Yes, performing on the "Great White Way" is the pinnacle, but success is just as great in other places. You can start in community theatre, where the house usually can hold anywhere from 25 to 75 people and you are a local celebrity. From there, regional theatre where you tour a certain area is the next step. Summer stock, where you can perform 6 different plays in as many weeks is a great training ground. Many great actors got their start off-Broadway, which is the general name given to smaller New York theatres. Touring companies of big Broadway shows let you play all of the big roles in a Broadway-size production and from there, the final step to Broadway is very short.

Life on the road

Actors are away from home much of the time. For a stage actor, working consistently means going to where the work is or, more precisely, going along with the work. For the big shows, this means a touring company, which brings everything with them and sets up in different cities. Depending on the length of stay, you may get an apartment with several other cast members, but more likely, you'll stay in a hotel while the show is running. Because theatre is a big deal in most small towns, you may do interviews on local radio and TV, talk to students in high school drama departments, and generally represent your production.

The pay

After you make the jump to professional theatre, you are eligible to join Actor's Equity, which is the union for stage actors and stage managers. Equity sets minimum wages for you and makes sure everything on the set is safe. The minimums change depending on the type of show you are in and where it is. If you are working in a small theatre with only a few hundred seats, you may only make $250 a week. If you are working in a big show on Broadway, your salary is $1,000 a week or more!

When do you work?

With few exceptions, plays start at 8:00 in the evening and finish around 10:30. How early you need to be there depends on your role in the play. You can get to the theatre as late as an hour before show time if you have a small part and don't require a lot of makeup or warm-up. If, however, you are starring in the play and need to wear gruesome makeup to make yourself look horrible, you'll probably need to get to the theatre early to be ready to go when the curtain rises.

During rehearsals though you will start work early in the day, just like a regular job, but you will work twice as long. In theatre, your job is to provide entertainment for people. Making it look easy is a lot of hard work.

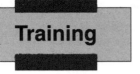

Training

Every actor has taken acting classes. A lot of actors, even after they become famous, continue to take classes so they will continue to learn. A good place to start is in school, where classes are free. Most high schools, even if they don't have a drama class, have a Drama Club you can join. In college, you can major in dramatic arts, and you'll be able to practice and learn and get a degree. After you decide to become a professional, you can take specialized classes for certain styles or methods of acting.

Now decide if dramatic acting is right for you

Dramatic actors have some special qualities. See if you can answer yes to the following questions.

Do you love a good death scene?

Can you quote Hamlet's soliloquy ("To be or not to be") in the shower?

Are you able to cry at the drop of a hat?

Can you make others cry at the drop of a hat?

Do you find yourself practicing dramatic poses?

Let's Meet...

Andrea Tate
Actress

Andrea has been involved in acting since she was little. Her dream is the same as it was then, to play Catwoman.

How did you get involved in acting?

I was an actress as a child, and a singer and dancer. I did some high school plays. But I didn't know that you could go study theatre. So I went to school for art. After I graduated I was working in New York as a commercial artist and I didn't like it. I quit my job and started waiting tables. I started meeting all these great people, and they were all out-of-work actors. So I asked them questions and they told me they were going to school for acting.

How did you get your first big break?

I was waiting tables and a customer, the artistic director for AMDA (American Musical Dramatic Academy) told me they were doing auditions for the school. I auditioned, got accepted, and began my training.

What do you like about acting?

The thing I like most about it is that you get to meet so many people. It's like a family every time you do a show. The audience comes to the theatre to sit there and be quiet and listen to you. They open themselves up to be vulnerable for whatever it is you're doing. I think acting pulls people together.

Is there anything you don't like about acting?

You have to have a second job, until you reach a certain point, so it can be frustrating.

Why did you move from New York to Los Angeles?

I started to get into another level where I was competing against big stars for off-Broadway roles. I can't compete against that, right now because nobody knows who Andrea Tate is. I decided to try LA for 6 months. Two and a half years later, I'm still here.

Where do you see yourself in 5 years?

I'm on a new campaign right now. I think my strong point is romantic drama. So in 5 years I'd like to be doing soap operas. I would be very happy with that schedule. My friends want to do features. Yeah, that would be good too, but to do soaps would be a blast for me.

What kind of advice would you give?

Go to the best schools you can. Find a really good coach you connect to.

How Andrea "Becomes" a Character

The first thing Andrea does is read the script three times in a relaxed state. This way she's really open to it and doesn't put any of her own ideas on it first. It's just neutral. After reading it three times, she starts to get an idea of what's happening.

Research is next. What were people's morals like at that time? What kind of clothes they wore affects the type of posture they had. What the weather was like affects what people were like. She spends a few days in the library getting answers to her questions. Then she goes through the script again and finds out what's happening in each one of the scenes. Then she starts to get a feel for the behavior of the character.

After that, she just keeps doing the behavior this character does. She does it throughout the day. If she's at home, she washes the dishes the way this person would wash the dishes. She walks down the street with this person's feeling in her body, so she starts to get a feeling for what this person is like. Then the character comes to her. Through the script, she gets little suggestions of what the person is like. Other characters also give her hints.

Let's Meet...

Scott Forrest
Actor

Scott enjoys all types of physical acting. He's even had a job where he got to beat up bad guys several times a day.

How did you get involved in acting?

I started when I was 8 or 9 years old in a play called "Penelope, Pride of the Pickle Factory." I'll never forget it. When I was 17, I headed down to LA and got in a play with Buddy Ebsen called "The Magnificent Yankee." From then on I just kept hitting plays and doing conservatory work. I worked at L.A. Actors Theatre.

Did you go to school for acting?

I wanted to be classically trained. To study with the best. I wanted a really good understanding of the stage. That's where it all began. I worked with Sandy Meisner, one of the gurus of the acting world, and with Stella Adler. I was lucky enough to study with people that pretty much are in the history books now.

Is Los Angeles a good place to work?

Los Angeles is such a wide, spread out place. You're not on the streets, walking around, heading to auditions, and in control. Everybody else has control. Deals tend to be made at pool parties or over the phone. It's been frustrating.

Where do you see yourself going from here?

I have so many interests. I'm interested in producing and directing, but at the same time, ultimately, for me it's still acting. I see myself creating projects and putting myself in them. Getting a movie machine, a production company that puts out stuff.

Do you prefer working on stage?

Love it. If I had to pick between the two, theatre and motion pictures, it's so tough. I was on a soundstage yesterday and when it all comes together and it all works, for one moment, it's a mindblower. Now in the theatre, you have the chance to get it right again and again, night after night.

What kind of advice would you give?

Be honest. It's your truth that's going to get you there. Stop comparing yourself with others.

Scott's Best Day as an Actor

Scott does very well with really accomplished, major directors. When he met Franco Zefferelli, Zefferelli was in the middle of rehearsal with 300 people around him. Scott knew he was just perfect for a part the famous director had been trying to cast for 6 weeks. Zefferelli whipped his head around, yelled out the character's name, and ran to Scott yelling, "Perfecto."

Scott says that when your instinct tells you it's going to work, you have to follow that completely. He auditioned for Zefferelli at the Metropolitan in New York and got into a production that aired on PBS television. He played the Prince of Persia and got the best review in the show from the *Village Voice* newspaper. It was a real awesome thing for Scott at the time.

Success Stories

James Earl Jones

The son of actor Robert Earl Jones, young James struggled with stuttering before finding his voice in drama. His Broadway debut came in 1958, and he won his first Tony Award 10 years later for *The Great White Hope.* Jumping easily between stage and screen, Mr. Jones has played Alex Haley in the TV miniseries *Roots* and is the voice of Darth Vader, villain of the *Star Wars* saga.

Glenn Close

Born in 1947, Glenn Close made her Broadway debut in 1974 in *Love for Love.* Even though she is best known for her work in film (*The Big Chill, Fatal Attraction*), she has won an Obie Award (for off-Broadway work) and two Tonys: one for portraying Annie in the American premiere of Tom Stoppard's *The Real Thing* and one for 1992's *Death and the Maiden.*

Find Out More

Your name in lights— on Broadway

It is the dream of all actors to one day appear on Broadway. If that is your dream, then you should check out the following places for information.

Bookstores are a great source of plays and texts on acting. Some, such as the Samuel French Bookstore, specialize in the dramatic arts.

Samuel French Bookstore
7623 Sunset Boulevard
Hollywood, CA 90046
(213) 876-0570

Colleges are the best place to learn and experiment with your craft.

University of Southern California
School of Performing Arts
University Park
Los Angeles, CA 90007
(213) 743-2235

Northwestern University
Evanston, IL 60201
(708) 492-7315

University of California, Los
    Angeles (UCLA)
Theater Arts Department
405 Hilgarde Avenue
Los Angeles, CA 90024
(310) 825-7891

New York University (NYU)
65 South Building
Washington Square
New York, NY 10003
(212) 598-3702

CAREERS IN MUSICAL THEATRE

In *Annie Get Your Gun* Ethel Merman sang, "There's no business like show business," and she was right. There's no feeling like waiting backstage, hearing the orchestra start the overture. You've already warmed up, and now you're waiting for the show to start. From behind, you watch the curtain rise. The stage lights glare into your face so you can't see the audience looking at you. The only thing you know is the music. In two bars you start: one, you open your mouth and two, begin to sing....

What it's like being a musical theatre performer

Imagine getting paid to do what most people do for free in the shower. Unless you're a rock star, the only place to do this is in musical theatre. Musical theatre itself is different from regular, dramatic acting. Musicals are the plays that most people remember and have the longest lives. In fact, the Tonys, which are the awards for Broadway shows, have a separate category for musicals. As a performer, being able to sing increases your chances of getting cast because more roles are available in musicals than in any other type of show.

Training

The best performers in musical theatre are what is known as "triple threats." This means they can do it all: act, sing, and dance. While it's not necessary to be able to do any of these to be a success, it certainly helps. To start, you should pick one area on which to focus. After you get good, you can start the second, then the third. In any case, starting out at school is the best bet. Chorus, drama, or dance classes are ways of getting a solid foundation for your work. Even things like cheerleading (for both boys and girls) can help with movement and voice.

Getting in the door

The key to starting any performing career is auditioning. An audition, technically speaking, is a trial performance. Basically, an audition is the time when you get to show your "stuff" to a director or choreographer. For musicals, you will be asked to bring in a prepared song, something similar to the style of music in the play, and to do a short dance sequence. Auditioning is not an easy thing to do, and the more you do it, the more relaxed you become. The more relaxed you are, the better your chances of getting cast. Besides, it's really hard to sing with a tight throat. A lot of singers will audition "just for experience" to make it easier for the parts they really want.

Climbing the career ladder

In musicals, the place to start is in the chorus. Like the chorus in school or church, in a musical, the chorus is a group of people singing together. The chorus provides the background singers and dancers for the main action. From the chorus, performers are chosen for bit parts, or solos. These are performers who stand out a little and are given their own credit line in the program. As you get notice in bit parts, you will move into featured roles where you play a specific character who is involved directly with the plot. While you work in the smaller roles, you may be given the opportunity to understudy a leading role. This means you get to perform when the leading performer is sick or takes the night off. From understudy, it's a short hop to where you are playing the lead yourself and others are understudying for you.

The rewards and the perks

The pay for musicals is very similar to the pay for dramatic actors because both are under Equity guidelines. The difference comes into play over a longer period of time. Musicals are more likely to tour than dramas, so as a performer you can extend your working life by going on the road. Also, because musicals contain something dramas do not, namely songs, there is always the possibility of a soundtrack album. Sometimes a song from a play will become a big hit on the radio, and if you are the person who sang it, that kind of exposure could lead to you getting a record contract.

Preparing to be a musical theatre performer

The best way to prepare for a career in musical theatre, beyond the training, is to know what you're getting into. First, see as many musicals as you can. Public television often carries Broadway shows and local schools and community theatres try to do at least one musical production a year. Second, go to the library and rent videos. Many, many musicals have been filmed directly from the stage productions or have been turned into movies. Third, listen to the soundtracks. Your neighborhood music store will have a soundtrack section, and all the ones you don't recognize are probably from Broadway or off-Broadway shows.

Do you have what it takes?

If you prefer to sing while explaining why you don't have your homework...

If dancing out of a room is the only way to leave it...

If you think Romeo and Juliet is a poor adaptation of *West Side Story*...

If Stephen Sondheim, Andrew Lloyd Webber, and Tim Rice sound vaguely familiar...

then musical theatre is right for you!

Let's Meet...

Veronica Armstrong
Actress and Singer

Day trips to Broadway in New York led Veronica to a life in the theatre.

How did you get involved in musical theatre?

I used to sing when I was younger. I was in a comedy first, and then I was in a musical a year later, in high school. It was choir first, chorus, and then acting.

What are the challenges of musical theatre?

There are certain challenges to singing and acting at the same time. There's a lot to do with breathing, you just need time to breathe sometimes. It's different than just acting because when you're acting there's a lot more you can do with your words than when you're singing because you have to sing a certain way. And it's a lot different than when you're singing because you have to do things with your body, your facial expressions. It's not like either of those kinds of performing, it's unique because it has combinations of both.

What kind of training do you need?

It can vary quite a bit. A lot of it will depend on your natural talents. Some people almost never need any vocal training. I would recommend that everyone have at least a little bit of training to learn how to warm up without damaging the vocal cords.

What about dancing?

Dancing...that's kind of interesting because I don't do it very well. The need for dancing ability varies from play to play. Some musicals don't have dancing, per se, but stage movement, more along the lines of walking to the right place at the right time and interacting with the other people on stage. People train a lot more for dancing. For musical theatre, you want to be able to do all that physical activity, which can be very draining, at the same time as singing and acting.

Is dancing important?

Actors need to know their abilities, know what they need to enhance, if they feel weak in a certain area. Not being able to dance should not keep you away from musical theatre. There's a lot there for nondancers as well.

Is there anything you don't like about musical theatre?

Musical theatre is a lot of work. Anything you do in a regular play is required of you when you do a musical piece, in addition to a lot of things that are physically draining. Even singing can be physically draining.

Veronica's Typical Show Day

You arrive. You have to warm up. The cast will usually warm up together. Lead actors may take more time for personal warm-up. You need to be in your costume or some sort of clothes for warm-up. Everybody arrives on the stage. Depending on the people involved, you might do physical warm-up first, or you might do vocal warm-up, but you definitely will do both.

Someone is usually in charge of the singers for vocal warm-up. It might not be the conductor, but someone who is there to work the singers in warm-up and practice. You usually work through vowel sounds, you want to work on consonant sounds to really get your mouth going. You have to really articulate in musical theatre, because words go by quickly, and they go by with instrumentation. All the parts of you that produce sound in singing have to be really fine-tuned, very accurate, so the audience can get as much of the sung text of the play as possible.

Then warming up all those muscles. Dancing, you warm up with simple stretches at first, then you start with the large muscle groups in a more vigorous manner. You'll most likely go through some of the dance segments of the play in your warm-up. You'll do group warm-up.

Then you get nervous and everybody gets ready for the beginning of the show.

Let's Meet...

Mike Wallis
Actor and Singer

Singing has always been natural to Mike, now he gets paid to do it.

What got you involved in musical theatre?

I always loved to sing, and I always loved musicals. I remember *Singing in the Rain* as one of my favorites. I always wanted to dance like Gene Kelly. It's fun because it incorporates so many styles; it incorporates acting, it incorporates comedy because most musicals have elements of humor in them, and singing, too. It's just a real rush being on a stage and singing a song and hearing the applause, especially if it's a showstopper.

What kind of training did you do?

Voice lessons are always important. I personally believe everyone can sing, just to varying degrees, and it helps to have a technique to fall back on. Stage movement is always good. Dancing. I'm not the greatest dancer, but I'm better than I was. That's really a lot of what you need as far as training goes.

What do you like best?

That's a tough call. If it's good music, fun music, I love that. It's fun to sing, fun to listen to. It's just a really special form of theatre having the audience be so immediate. More so than a dramatic play because in musicals people will stop and applaud regularly after songs. In a drama or a comedy you don't usually get that, they usually wait until the end of the act.

Is there anything you don't like?

Depending on certain pieces, the costumes. Sometimes, if it's a song you don't particularly care for, that's not a lot of fun. You have to do it the best you can, but if it's a song you don't really have a connection with, that's kind of difficult. The choreography is tough. It's fine after you do it, but learning to do it is tough.

Where do you see yourself in 5 years?

I see myself on the big screen. Doing musicals, occasionally. There's not a big call for musicals in film, but I do believe there's an avenue, a need people may not know of yet, but they will. One day, soon, musicals will make a comeback and I'll be waiting. People just don't know what they're missing.

What advice would you give?

Learn your craft, as with anything. Take voice lessons. Take dancing and movement because the more you have, the easier it is when it finally happens.

Mike Describes an Audition

The audition, even though it's a work in progress, is the place to shine.

You bring in a piece of music, sometimes you can sing a cappella, but they prefer you use an accompanist just to make sure that you can sing with music. Bring in something close to musical theatre. It doesn't have to be a piece from musical theatre, but don't come in singing "Black Dog." They want to see what you can do on your own, and if you're close to getting it, then they'll say "He's close to getting it and we can work with him."

If they like the way you sing, they'll have you read. You'll read a piece from the play, a nonsinging part.

Then you'll do a choreography thing just to make sure you know your right foot from your left. They'll bring in a choreographer to do a piece of choreography with all the people they are interested in.

Then you wait. Usually you'll get a call in the next day or two to let you know if you got the part.

Success Stories

Tommy Tune

Born Thomas James Tune in 1939, Tune made his Broadway debut at the age of 26 in the chorus of *Baker Street*. He quickly became well known as a dancer and choreographer, and in 1973 brought the house down with his clog dancing in *Seesaw*. Tune is the only person to win Tony Awards (the awards for Broadway performances) in four different categories: Featured Actor (*Seesaw*), Choreographer (*A Day in Hollywood/A Night in the Ukraine*), Director (*Nine*), and Leading Actor (*My One and Only*).

Bernadette Peters

Bernadette Peters made her Broadway debut at the age of 11 with the 1959 revival of *The Most Happy Fella*. From there, she received critical acclaim for her work in shows like *Dames at Sea, Sunday in the Park with George,* and *Into the Woods.* She won a Tony in 1985 for her performance in *Song and Dance.* Ms. Peters has also appeared in several major motion pictures.

Mandy Patinkin

Imagine not singing until college, then your first time out in a musical, you not only land the lead role, but win a Tony for your efforts! That's what happened to Mandy Patinkin when he starred as Ché in *Evita*. Never one to rest, Patinkin has jumped back and forth between Broadway and film starring in everything from *Yentl* and *Sunday in the Park with George* to *Alien Nation* and his own one-man show, *Mandy Patinkin in Concert: Dress Casual.*

Find Out More

You and musical theatre

Is performing in a musical right for you? How do you know? Ask yourself these questions.

Can I read music?

Do I like to sing?

Is chorus one of my favorite classes?

Do I like to practice scales?

Do I enjoy sitting around singing more than I enjoy watching TV?

Did you answer yes? Then maybe it's time to look into singing lessons and finding a local theatre holding auditions for the next musical.

CAREERS IN SKETCH COMEDY

A s an actor, your greatest challenge is creating unique characters. Imagine the fun of being able to create a half dozen or more different characters, all playing different roles, in an evening. How about putting these characters into a dozen "miniplays" a night? Now imagine that all of these characters have one thing in common: They make people laugh. This is the world of sketch comedy, where changing a character is as easy as changing your clothes.

What it's like to do sketch comedy

For the most part, when you perform sketch comedy, you work with someone else, either a single partner or as part of a troupe. As a performer, you are often also responsible for writing your own material. A show has as many as 25 sketches in a row (separated by blackouts or pre-taped short films, themselves taken from sketches) and is under the control of a single director. When you do a show, you spend a lot of time changing clothes. Sometimes you will have to put on seven or eight different costumes or wigs for one performance, and when you do two performances a night, that's a lot of changing.

History of sketch comedy

Sketches have been entertaining people for hundreds of years. Burlesque shows in the Wild West were all sketch shows with some music thrown in. In the early part of this century, vaudeville relied heavily on sketch comedy. Comedy groups like the Marx Brothers, Abbott and Costello, and the Three Stooges, which later became famous in movies, all started out doing short sketches. Even television has done a number of sketch comedy shows, from Sid Caesar's "Your Show of Shows" to "Saturday Night Live." Sketch comedy is still going strong.

What is a sketch?

According to the dictionary, a sketch is a short, often satirical scene or play in a revue or variety show; a skit. Sketches are different from plays in several ways. First of all, they are much shorter. A play is usually 2 hours long and divided into acts, while a sketch is not more than a few minutes. A play generally uses scenery designed for the show, but a sketch show has to have a set that is multipurpose. Finally, a play can be funny or serious, comedy or drama, but sketches are always funny.

Preparing to do sketch comedy

The best way to prepare to perform sketch comedy is to go to school. A lot of top professionals in the field started out doing skits with some friends in high school or college and made their way into bigger, better-paying troupes. However, if you don't want to experiment, many of the top sketch comedy groups in the country also offer classes. These classes will teach you the principles of how to quickly create a character, how to write for yourself, and how to improvise. Improvisation, which is the ability to think on your feet and make up things as you go, is very important in sketch comedy.

Training

At The Groundling Theatre, home of the Groundlings, one of the most well-known sketch comedy groups in the country, you have to audition just to join the school. After you're in (which requires you know a little bit about theatre), you start in the Basic Class. After 12 meetings, if your teacher thinks you are ready, you get promoted into the Intermediate Class. These first two levels teach you how to be loose on stage and how to improvise. If you get promoted to the next level, the Writing Lab, you spend 6 weeks working on writing sketches. Advanced Class is the next, and final, level of the school's regular classes. After Advanced, the students who have made it perform for a minimum of six months in "The Sunday Show." After proving themselves as writers and performers, a select few are asked to join The Groundlings Company. It is a very big honor to make it into the regular performing troupe and often takes more than 3 years of hard work.

How do you know you're doing a good job?

The easiest way to know you are doing a good job is to listen. For an actor, listening is very important, but in this instance you are not listening to the other actors on stage, you are listening to the audience. When a sketch blacks out and it's time for you to go backstage and prepare for your next scene, if the audience applauds wildly, then you know you've done a good job. If, while you are performing, you have to stop and wait for the laughter to die down, you know you are a success.

The pleasures and pressures of the job

Some of the pleasures of performing in a sketch comedy show are that you are constantly creating. Every time you write a sketch it is an opportunity to try something new, create a new character, or see what a different situation would be like. Even if it doesn't go well, it's okay. It's only a few minutes before you're offstage and again waiting for your turn to go back out and perform a different character in a new setting. Of course, if the audience is bad, then nothing you do may make them laugh. This can be upsetting sometimes, but remember, after this audience leaves, another one will come in, and you can start over.

Decide if sketch comedy is right for you

Do you like to make people laugh?

Do you like to dress up in different clothes and talk in strange accents?

Is it fun to pretend you're another person, just for a little while?

Do you make up stories to amuse your parents and friends?

Do you act out scenes from movies and play all the parts, or get your friends to help you?

If you answered yes to even one of these questions, you may have a calling in sketch comedy.

Let's Meet...

Peggy Maltby
Sketch Comic

Peggy has been doing sketch comedy for 12 years, and she wouldn't have it any other way.

How did you get involved with sketch comedy?

I went to see a friend perform and thought "This is what I want to do."

What kind of training do you have?

I was a drama major in college, I went to two acting conservatories after college. With that as a foundation, when you're doing sketch comedy it gives you a broader base, a broader understanding of style, of timing, of what's important in a scene.

What do you like best about doing sketch comedy?

The risks involved. To poke fun at the basics, really.

Is there anything you don't like about sketch comedy?

That it doesn't always get the respect it deserves. People don't understand how hard it is.

What kind of advice would you give to people starting out?

They need to be well read. They need to observe what goes on in the world. A lot of sketch comedy is satire. You need to know what's going in the headlines so you can write about that.

Do you prefer to work by yourself?

I definitely prefer other actors on stage because then you have the dynamic of working off someone. It's not always going to be the same. When you're working with just yourself, you can sometimes get lost in your own head. With other actors on stage, you have to be aware of yourself, you have to be aware of them. You have to listen.

Do you prefer sketch comedy to regular theatre?

I like both because both offer a different set of rewards. Sketch comedy is like a sprint runner and doing a full-length production is like running the marathon. They both are gratifying but in different ways.

Do you see yourself doing this in 5 years?

Yes. Sketch comedy can have all ages involved in it. Even when I'm 80 I can still be writing and performing.

How Peggy Writes a Sketch

Initially, if something strikes you as funny, you can say "Why is this funny?" It could be that you recognize yourself in this situation. It could be that it's so absurd. The idea has to be something you feel strongly about.

Then, after you decide, "I want to write a sketch about making an omelette," you have to then ask "What's my POV, my point of view."

After that is established, you can decide who else is going to be in the scene, how it will start, what the middle transition will be, and how it will end. Then write it and see if that's where it goes.

Sometimes you'll think "Okay, these are my beats, my beginning, middle, and end," and you write the beginning, you get to the middle, and you realize the end you were heading toward is not the end that is developing. Then you have to choose to go with the end that is developing or rewrite the middle to get the end you want.

Then you perform it. Sometimes during the rehearsal process, you have to be willing to change because after you've added other actors, they may have improvements. So you have to be willing to let go.

Let's Meet...

Phil La Marr
Sketch Comic

Phil loves all the acting he's done for film and TV and stage, but was most excited when a part he played was mentioned in a comic book.

How did you get involved in sketch comedy?

I got involved in sketch comedy through improvisation I'd done in college and in Chicago.

Has being able to improvise helped your acting?

Yes. Generally, acting is improvisation. The difference being how much. In a regular improvisation, you have to make up the dialogue, make up the space you're in and you're only given, say, your job. You have that one thing you're given and you make everything else up. In regular acting, you're given everything else; who you are, what you have to say, but you still have to improvise how to say it, where you move, when you say it.

What do you like most about acting?

I enjoy the relationship with the audience in live acting. The challenge of making something come to life.

Have you always wanted to be an actor?

No. I think I always have been an actor. I was a very serious child, although I made people laugh. So I just gravitated toward my natural tendencies.

What kind of advice would you give to someone starting out?

Get as many different influences as you can. Acting and performing, especially comedy, is so much about getting back to what you were as a four- or five-year-old. You can tell a four-year-old "You're a fire chief, go!" That's all they need. We all have all the information that we'll ever need to make something up, or to act something. It's all inside us. We just have to get used to bringing it out.

Where do you get ideas for sketches?

From a lot of different places. Something that makes me angry. Driving or a story in the newspaper. "How can people think like this?" Then my mind starts going, and I write a sketch of someone who thinks that way.

Phil's First Performance

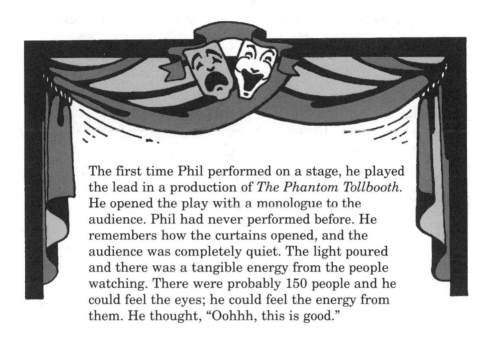

The first time Phil performed on a stage, he played
the lead in a production of *The Phantom Tollbooth*.
He opened the play with a monologue to the
audience. Phil had never performed before. He
remembers how the curtains opened, and the
audience was completely quiet. The light poured
and there was a tangible energy from the people
watching. There were probably 150 people and he
could feel the eyes; he could feel the energy from
them. He thought, "Oohhh, this is good."

Success Stories

Phil Hartman started his career in sketch comedy as a second career. He was already successful as a graphic designer and had even designed the covers of some very popular record albums when he decided to try out for The Groundlings. He was accepted, went through the whole program, and was eventually asked to join the company. In 1984, Hartman wrote and starred in a play that was presented as part of the arts celebration at the Olympics. He later joined the cast of "Saturday Night Live" and then made the jump into feature films.

Listening to universal advice to "have something to fall back on," Lisa Kudrow graduated from Vassar College with a degree in biology before pursuing a performing career. She joined the cast of the Groundling Theatre, where she was a regularly performing member, in 1990. Since then, she has skyrocketed to fame playing all sorts of ditzy roles on various TV shows, including "Friends."

Dan Aykroyd

Dan Aykroyd is a native Canadian who was one of the original cast members of "Saturday Night Live." He started out with Second City, a famous and very popular sketch comedy troupe in Toronto, where he learned quite a bit about writing. He learned so much about writing he won an Emmy in 1977 for some of his sketches on "Saturday Night Live."

Find Out More

Sketch Comedy and You

To find out more about Sketch Comedy, watching TV shows like *Saturday Night Live, Fridays,* and *The Carol Burnett Show* is the best place to start. Once you decide you'd like to try it on your own, look in your local yellow pages for theatres near you, and contact them for information on classes and performance schedules. Here are the addresses and phone numbers for some of the most well-known comedy theatres in the country. If you live near one of them, they'd be a great place to get started.

The Groundlings
7307 Melrose Ave.
Hollywood, CA 90038
(213) 934-9700

Second City
1616 N. Wells
Chicago, IL 60614
(312) 642-6514

Acme Comedy Theatre
1335 N. La Brea Ave.
Hollywood, CA 90038
(213) 525-0202

CAREERS IN STUNT WORK

Someone's shooting at you. You turn and run, dodging the bullets that explode around you. You run faster, jumping high into the air to somersault into the stack of cardboard. Then, without warning, the palette the boxes are on lifts high into the air. You are now 50 feet above the ground. A shot rings out! You're hit! You stagger and fall off the platform into the pool of water below. As you resurface, gasping for air, you hear the wild applause of the audience watching the stunt show.

What it's like to be a stunt performer

Performing stunts is the most physically demanding of all the performing arts. In film, a stunt person will come in and replace the featured actor just for the stunt. There are few times in theatre when a stunt is too dangerous for an actor to perform. In a stunt show, however, the actors must all be stunt people. One 20-minute show can have as many as 50 stunts. A stunt performer must be in great physical and mental shape in order to complete these stunts several times a day.

The pleasures and pressures of the job

The pleasures of being a stunt performer are harder to define than the pressures. While you may work for only 20 minutes every hour and a half, it's a hard 20. You work outside and you perform for hundreds of people a day, but you always have to practice your craft. The possibility of making a mistake is greater in a stunt show than in a regular play, and if you make a mistake, it could be very dangerous. It's quite possible for a stunt performer to break a bone during a show.

The rewards and the perks

Stunt shows are fast becoming one of the most popular attractions in the country. Stunt shows are appearing at a lot of the new theme parks all over the world. Even places like Sea World have a water-skiing stunt show. Being a stunt performer, you can take full advantage of this and get a job anywhere in the country. Often, stunt people use their experience to get them work as a stage actor in a more mainstream play. If you know how to fake a fistfight, you have an advantage over an untrained actor in roles that call for stage combat.

The pay

Being a stunt show performer pays well and regularly. In film, stunt people are paid by the stunt, depending on its difficulty. A high fall is paid by the foot. But working in a film means you may do only one stunt and then not work for a few weeks. When you perform with a stunt show, you get a weekly paycheck and (depending on where you work) benefits. You also know where you're going to be working, so you don't have to worry about travelling to a film location. If you have a very nice boss, you probably will even get the chance to work on movies, as long as you don't miss too many days of work.

Climbing the career ladder

There are different kinds of stunts, and as you progress in the field, generally you will get better at one type over another. When starting out, you'll learn the basics, like how to fake hitting someone or being hit. In a show, you will be given smaller roles as "bad guy #2" where you'll be in a few fights and maybe get hit by a fake bullet. When you learn how to do a high fall, your director will incorporate that into the show. As you get better, you'll learn more. Eventually, you will become the featured performer in the show. At that point, you will start to talk with your director and plan certain stunts. Eventually, you could become a director yourself, coordinating a complete stunt show and helping to train younger stunt people.

Training

Being a stunt performer requires you to be in the best physical shape you can be in because you are pushing your body very hard. The more you know, the better equipped you'll be. If you can learn physiology, how the body works, you'll know more about how to train yourself. You should also get as much aerobic exercise as possible. Riding your bike everyday is a good way to start. Learning martial arts or gymnastics is a solid foundation. More advanced studies like stage combat, fencing, and dance will get you further along. When you're ready to go for a career, there are stunt schools where you are taught the basics and more specialized schools where you can learn things like stunt driving or horsemanship. If you are a specialist in any dangerous field (mountain climbing, sky-diving) you can also get work performing stunts in those areas. That last kind of specialty, how-ever, is primarily for movies or TV only.

Now decide if stunt work is right for you

Make a list of what kinds of activities you think are fun. If your fun list includes things like playing sports, white-water rafting, mountain biking, surfing, or tree climbing, then you might want to think about stunt work.

Now make a list of your favorite TV shows and movies. Do you have shows with Steven Seagal, Harrison Ford, Jean-Claude Van Damme, Sylvester Stallone, Arnold Schwarzenegger, Richard Dean Anderson, or any-thing written by Stephen J. Canell? If so, you'll definitely want to look into stunt work.

Let's Meet...

Bonzai Vitale
Stuntman

Bonzai has been falling out of, off of, and into things for the past 10 years.

How did you get involved in stunt work?

I always wanted to do stunt work after I saw my first movie. I watched it and I knew. Those dudes getting beat up and falling off things, that's what I wanted to do. All through high school I did everything I could to prepare myself. I flew ultralights, rode motorcycles, worked out, sky-dived. I took pole vaulting for 4 years to build up my coordination and air sense. Looking back on it, I wish I'd done gymnastics as well.

What do you like most about doing stunt work?

Creating the illusion. I love fooling people. I love it when someone comes up to me and asks "Man, does that hurt when he hits you in the face?" It's different in live shows. You can do a lot more illusion with film and TV than you can with a live show. There's usually not the

money to do it, and you can't use camera tricks.

Is there anything you don't like?

Getting in with people who haven't been in the business a long time or think they know about stunt work. Sometimes actors come in and they won't take direction. You find yourself keeping a watchful eye to make sure you don't get hurt or clipped or something.

What do you see yourself doing in 5 years?

I want to be stunt coordinating feature films. Eventually work into second unit directing. Stunt work is what I do. I never considered myself an actor. I'm a stuntman with some ability to act. I can say a few lines and be convincing before I'm blown out a window or something, but acting doesn't do a whole lot for me. Stunt work is what I really love, it's what gives me the rush.

What advice would you give to someone starting out?

Listen to people who have been in the business. Listen and learn. If you go out on a set, don't talk, just listen. Most of everything I learned is just by watching the old-timers and listening to them talk. Usually people are pretty cool, they'll come up and talk to you and then you can ask a few questions. And always remember that safety is of number one importance, over everything. <u>Everything.</u>

Bonzai Masters High Falls

Bonzai did a 70-foot, back, high fall for "Eyewitness News." It took him 4 years of hard work to get up to that level, starting out at lower levels.

With high falls, one mistake and you can really, really get hurt. A late tuck and you'll break your neck. An over rotation and you'll break your neck. If you miss your mark, you're going to slam your heels or your head on the concrete. So many things can go wrong.

People say, "I want to do a high fall," and when they look at it, they say, "Oh, it's not that high, it can't be that hard," but guys have gotten killed on 10-foot falls.

To learn, you need to find somebody who's good at high falls. The process is a slow, step-by-step process. You always have someone supervising you. Each time you get a fall right two or three times in a row, you move up a little higher. Pretty soon, you work your way up until you're competent to do the higher falls.

Let's Meet...

Casi Smith

Stuntwoman

Casi enjoys doing things that excite her and embarrass her parents. She still can't believe she gets paid for it.

How did you get involved in stunt work?

I heard about the audition through a friend, and I thought it would be exciting and adventurous. I'm basically athletic and I like that kind of physicality and performance, so I went to the audition. I got the job, then when this current show opened, I auditioned for it. Stunt work isn't anything I thought I would get into.

What do you like about doing stunt work?

You get a good workout without really trying. I love the fantasy, pulling the audience into the story line, and the make-believe aspect of it all. They're here to be entertained, and stunt shows are definitely entertaining. Stunt shows are not just performing on stage and throwing out lines. It's pyrotechnics and stunts and comedy.

Do you enjoy working with the audience?

I love working with the audience. And the
"meet and greets" afterwards, dealing with
the kids, when they get to shake hands
with you, there's nothing better than that.

Is there anything you don't like?

I don't like getting hurt. Last year I got
hurt all the time. I always had bruises and
cuts on my legs. I tore my hamstring. This
year it's not as physical, so I haven't gotten
hurt. But it can be grueling. The heat can
really be hard on the human body. It can
get really hard to breathe, especially
running around.

What did you do to prepare?

I had to do a lot of training. I took judo and
karate years ago, and I had to retrain
myself. This year, the high fall definitely
was a major thing to accomplish. It scared
me to death. I fall about 12 feet, which
doesn't sound like very far. To jump feet
first into a lake or something is nothing,
but this, you're falling on your back on a
hard mat. To fall on your back, you have to
have a feel, in the air, of where you are so
you land flat. You can get the air knocked
out of you if you don't do it right.

What Makes Casi's Day

Casi does five shows a day. It can be tough, especially in the heat. She also does the pre-show, to get the audience going. There are plenty of times that she doesn't feel up to it and before she comes out, the cast and the crew have to pump her up. They clap and cheer for her and that helps a lot. What really makes it good is when she has an excellent audience response. A dead audience can break the show.

Casi remembers some shows she didn't think would be good and she came out and the audience was just fantastic. It wasn't necessarily a show where she was just perfect on everything—maybe she was a little bit off, but she overcame that and made it work. Pulling it all together and making it work, and sticking to the soundtrack, is a great feeling for Casi. She also loves the "meet and greet." The little kids are just in awe. They just want to touch her and they kiss Batman, and she can see their excitement in their eyes. That makes it all worthwhile.

Success Stories

Burt Reynolds

A famous story is told on the Universal Studios Tour about a young stuntman who flubbed a scene in a film. The director was so upset he told the stuntman he "would never work in Hollywood again." Today, no one remembers who the director was, but the stuntman was Burt Reynolds, who went on to become one of the biggest movie stars in the world. Some of Reynolds' biggest films were based around great stunts, and *Hooper,* which came out in the late 70s, is a great film about a stuntman.

Hal Needham started out as a stuntman, became a second-unit director, then teamed up with Burt Reynolds to create *Smokey and the Bandit,* one of the biggest blockbusters of all time. During the course of his career, Needham directed some of the most stunt-intensive films ever made. He went on to help invent the Shotmaker, a truck specifically designed to make it easier to film a moving car.

Find Out More

What It Takes To Be a Stunt Performer

Read the following sentences and rate each one from 1 to 5, with 1 meaning "strongly disagree" and 5 meaning "strongly agree."

I like physical activities. ____

I am not afraid of heights. ____

I always stretch before I work out. ____

Going fast does not bother me. ____

I can take direction well. ____

I am very precise and like to practice things I enjoy. ____

I like performing. ____

Working with other people is something I enjoy. ____

Now add up your score and see if stunt work is right for you.

30-40	Future stunt person
20-29	Definite stunt possibilities
10-19	Stunt watcher
0-9	Stunt avoider

CAREERS IN PLAYWRIGHTING AND DIRECTING

Y ou're sitting in the back row of the audience as the lights start to dim. After a brief anticipation in the darkness, the stage lights begin to glow. When they reach full brightness, you can see the actors on stage. They begin talking, but you don't need to hear them to know what they're saying. You know the words well. You wrote them yourself months, even years ago. Finally, you watch with pride as the actors take their bows, and you know you did a good job.

Why make the jump to writer?

As an actor, you are under the control of a variety of things. You have to say the words that are written, and you have to say them the *way* the director wants you to, *where* he wants you to. Sometimes actors want to take some of that control back, so they become playwrights and directors themselves. This way, if you have something you want to say, you can say it. Often, an actor will write a play just to get themselves seen. In larger cities, like Los Angeles and New York, where thousands of struggling actors are auditioning for every small part, it's easier to write a part for yourself, which you know you are right for, than it is to try out for someone else's plays.

The rewards and the perks

Like all creative works, the rewards vary. For a lot of people, the biggest reward is just having people come and see your work. There is the satisfaction of having your thoughts and ideas expressed in a public forum. Of course, there's also the money. When a play is successful, not only will you make money from its run, you can sell the rights to produce it to other people. Special agencies, like Samuel French, are play publishers and will administer your plays when theatre companies and high schools around the country want to mount them in their own seasons. Additionally, after you have written one successful play, it is easier to sell your next one. Movie and TV companies look for young playwrights to write films and TV shows.

What it's like to be a writer/director

The writer and the director have the ultimate power in the theatre. In a movie, the stars may change their dialogue or the producer can tell the director what to do, but not in theatre. The writer, especially on a new play, works with the director throughout the entire rehearsal process. If a line or scene doesn't work, the writer and director discuss it, and a new scene is written.

What a director does

A director is responsible for everything that the audience sees and hears from the time the stage lights go up to the time the audience leaves. The director has final approval of all designs and will have dozens of meetings with the design staff during preproduction. The main thing the director does is work with the actors. A director will read a script several times and, if possible, discuss it with the writer. After the director has an idea of what the play is "about," the subtext, the director will lead the actors to the same conclusions. By guiding the actors into different emotions, the director will bring about the full story.

The writer's job

Everything starts with the writer's idea. "What happens when...?" leads to an answer, then to a story, then eventually to a play. The writer needs to research the topic to portray it as accurately as possible. Sometimes, the research shapes the story. After the story is roughly sketched out, all the plot points resolved, then the writer creates characters to tell the story. With the characters comes the writing of dialogue with speech patterns and dialects. You have to be able to tell your story almost entirely with words. The actors and director will take it from there and make it come alive.

Preparing to be a writer or a director

Starting out as an actor is a good way, if not the best, to prepare to be a writer or a director. After you know how it feels to be on stage, you have a better understanding of how to make the stage say what you want it to. As an actor, you will be exposed to different styles of theatre, especially if you take theatre courses in school. As you read and perform plays, you will be able to get an idea of how dialogue works, how sentences sound when spoken aloud, and how they are different than sentences that are read. You can take all of these lessons and apply them to your own work when you need to write a scene or explain to an actor how you want the actor to move.

Getting a head start

Aside from reading as many plays as you can, a good way to start is to just do it. The next time you read a book, find your favorite scene. Then turn it into a dialogue scene. Write the description of the setting in terms of what can be seen on the stage, describe the characters' actions as they enter or move around the set, then put in the dialogue. It's okay if it doesn't match exactly what's in the book, the point is to get the idea across. Now take the scene and ask a few of your acting friends to perform it for you. Help them out with direction. After a few scenes like this, you can start creating your own scenes, then a full play will follow.

Let's Meet...

William Schreiner
Director

William has directed for stage and screen for more than 15 years. He even directed his son in a film.

Why did you make the jump from acting into writing and directing?

I got lucky at an acting audition for a soap opera and that started a 10-year acting career, but I actually always wanted to direct.

Did you go through any special training to become a director?

I was in one play (in college) and was very attracted to what the director was doing. I thought, "You know, I want to do that." So I turned around and directed a play immediately after that. It was a big success in school and I thought, "I guess I can do this." I continued to direct plays and went to graduate school. I got a master of fine arts degree in directing.

What makes a good director?

The best directors are those who have done some acting themselves. They know how to communicate with actors, and

understand the kinds of problems actors have. Having that experience, I can help an actor make a performance happen.

What do you like about being a director?

I like the creative process. I like being able to bring out the best in actors and to bring a unique experience and vision for an audience. I like taking chances.

What is the most difficult part of your job?

Casting is the toughest thing. When you read a play you get a sense of the "inner tick" of each individual character. Then you look for actors that bring, by nature, something that resonates with you as far as the "tick" of that particular character. In stage, you're also looking for people that will add things to your vision of the character that perhaps you hadn't thought of before but when you see them, when you hear the words, you realize there's an enhancement to what's just there on the page.

What do you prefer to direct?

Generally, I prefer comedy. There's something satisfying in putting something together and seeing that you did tickle people.

William's Advice

- Read as many scripts as possible so you're familiar with what's out there. Stay very up on what's going on in the current theatre scene.

- Experience as much as possible. Try other skills, crafts, and arts that are involved with putting a play together. Assist a lighting designer if you can, take an acting class, write a play.

- Remember, they call it a play. It's all playing. It's letting your imagination build an alternate reality that exists for 2 hours in the presence of an audience. In some ways it's not that much different from handing a little kid Legos. Most kids will tell you it's more fun to play with a hundred pieces of Legos with different shapes than it is to play with two or three of the same color and shape. It's just the more you have to play with, the more fun it is.

- A director's job is part cheerleader, part disciplinarian, and part visionary. I always think of a director as leading a group of people into the darkness. The director is the one holding the only flashlight. A director has to have a sense of where to go but also how to look for the things that people will all discover they need in order to make the thing work.

Let's Meet...

Deanna Oliver
Writer

Deanna has written "Animaniacs" on TV and *Casper* at the movies. She writes with a partner.

How did you start writing?

I performed with a sketch comedy group that required you to write your own material, your own sketches, your own little monologues. My sketches were pretty successful. So that's when I decided that I could write.

What do you like/dislike about writing?

I like the creativity, the hours. I like the ability to bring characters to life.

Sometimes the rewrite process can get hairy if 20 different people are giving you notes and ideas, and you have your own. It can get frustrating and difficult. That's completely out-balanced by your own creativity and what you can do on your own.

Is there any special training?

I think a good education is very important. I think you have to go to college. I think you take English and literature classes, I

think you should read the classics. I think
you should read all the plays you can get a
hold of. If you want to write you have to
read. You have to read everything, all
kinds of everything.

Where do you see yourself in 5 years?

Directing movies. That would be fun, and
it would probably be a movie that I had
written with my partner. We'll probably
team up to produce and direct our own.
That'd be a blast, because I love directing,
too. Even more than acting. It didn't start
out that way.

How did you get involved in theatre?

When I was six there was a Christmas
pageant, and they told me I was going to
be in the chorus, and I said "No, I'm
Raggedy Ann. I'm not going to play
Raggedy Ann, I *am* Raggedy Ann." This is
true. My hero was Bette Davis. I used to
watch old Bette Davis movies.

What's the difference between writing a stage play and a movie?

Length. Shots. A play can be less action
and more dialogue. A play can be more
symbolic. I prefer movies, because I understand them better. I like the form. You can
go to any location. You can do that in
theatre, too, it's just different.

How Deanna Wrote Her Play

Deanna's play, "Holiday Dinner," was based on a sketch done with two other people. Deanna was the one at the keyboard, and was the one responsible for structure. That was her first play so she had to learn a lot. She read books on how to write a play. She knew a lot of plays. Today she would write it completely differently. It was a process, a learning, growing thing. The play was critically successful. It had a lot of heart and comedy to it. Because she was writing and acting, during rehearsals she would have a keyboard on the stage, and she would run over and change a line right then and there. It didn't help her acting, but it helped her writing. It took her a while longer to learn how to act in that play because she was so busy writing it. Literally, in rehearsals she would be writing, which means she was not really involved in her character because she was looking at the whole.

Success Stories

Born in Detroit in 1939, young Mary Jean "Lily" Tomlin had no idea she would win a Tony Award for Best Actress in 1985. Lily first came to the public eye when she joined the cast of TV's "Laugh-In" in 1969, but it was her stage work where she really shined. She cowrote two one-woman shows (*Appearing Nitely* and *The Search for Signs of Intelligent Life in the Universe,* for which she won the Tony); both enjoyed long runs on Broadway. Ms. Tomlin has created many characters, like Ernestine the telephone operator, which have become identifiable all over the world.

Chazz Palmenteri

Chazz Palmenteri is an actor who had a story to tell. When he told it, the result was *A Bronx Tale,* a one-person, semi-autobiographical play originally produced in Los Angeles. *A Bronx Tale* led Palmenteri to Broadway and eventually to films, where he wrote the screen adaptation as well as played one of the major roles opposite Robert DeNiro. Chazz also starred in Woody Allen's film *Bullets over Broadway,* in which he played a writer.

Find Out More

Do you have a future in writing or directing?

Being a writer or a director is hard work. Answer the following questions to see if it's something you'd like to pursue.

Do you like to create stories about people and things?

Do you like to boss people around?

Do you like to work with other creative people?

Is reading near the top of your list of things to do?

Can you type?

Do you like to write?

When you look at a picture, do you notice the details?

Are you involved in drama already?

Do you enjoy seeing plays?

A group of "yes" answers could mean you are meant to be behind the spotlight, writing and directing the stars.

CAREERS

BACKSTAGE

B efore the audience comes in and after it leaves, a lot of work has to be done. While the actors are putting on their makeup or taking their bows, a whole crew of people is working to make sure the show goes off without a hitch. While the star is delivering her lines, trained technicians are making sure that she can be seen and heard. This is the backstage technical crew, and without it, theatre couldn't exist.

What it's like to work backstage

Working backstage is hard work. No matter the size of the show, you will have props that need to be placed in the proper area before and during the show so the actors know where they are at all times. You may be needed to help change someone's costume or even to rearrange the set. Working in the technical booth is also considered backstage work even though the booth is usually in front of the stage. Depending on the size of your production, the people in the booth handle everything from running the light and sound boards and the spotlight to giving cues to all of the people on the crew.

Getting a head start

Working backstage, or being a "techie," is the easiest way to get started in the theatre. No matter where you live, you can get involved in productions, either with your school, church/temple, or a community theatre. To get involved, all you have to do is express an interest. Most theatres are very happy to have volunteers helping to build sets, paint scenery, and take tickets. Any courses you can take in school about theatre will only help, as will shop classes. Knowing how to weld, saw, hammer, and glue are definite advantages.

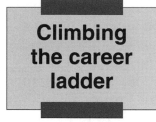

Climbing the career ladder

In theatre, you learn best by doing. Here's an idea of how you progress:

General stage crew—moving scenery, runner, set construction, and strike

Rail—working the rope system that raises and lowers scenery (in larger theatres)

Department assistant—working in the prop, costume, or technical department; helping as a dresser or in presetting the stage props

Department head—being in charge of a department

Board operator—running a light or sound board

Assistant stage manager—overseeing the backstage crew, helping the stage manager

Stage manager—running the day-to-day operations of the show

Director—the person in charge

The only thing not listed is designer. The designer (set, costume, lighting) is the person responsible for the look of the show. While you can work your way up to these positions, it is best to go to school specifically to study a particular area.

The rewards and the perks

Sometimes the rewards of working in the theatre can be financial. If you become a member of Equity (the stage performers union that also covers stage crew) and work on an Equity show, you can make a lot of money. However, most people who find work in technical theatre do it for other reasons. You can make a living working backstage, but a lot of people do it just for fun. In community theatre, people work as a family to "put on a show." Sometimes you put in time as a techie because you didn't get cast in the show. Sometimes you do it to meet people who have similar interests. Sometimes you do it because listening to an audience applaud and knowing you were a part of what brought them joy is the greatest feeling in the world.

When you work

Theatre work is different from a regular job. When you're building a set, you work normal hours, but when the show is running, you have to go to work just when most people are coming home.

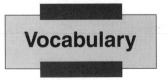

Here are some useful theatre terms to know backstage:

House—where the audience sits

Upstage—the end of the stage furthest away from the audience

Downstage—the end of the stage closest to the audience

Stage right—the left side of the stage from the audience perspective

Stage left—the right side of the stage from the audience perspective

Prop—anything an actor carries on stage

Costume—anything an actor wears on stage

Instrument—a device used to light the stage

Light—what an instrument produces

Cue—the signal to perform an action (i.e., change the lighting when the actor moves downstage)

Intermission—the break between acts

Places—the house is in, and it's time to get ready to start the show.

Let's Meet...

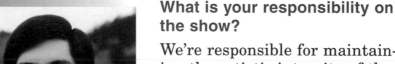

David Lober
Stage Manager

David has spent 12 years working backstage on some of the biggest, and some of the smallest, shows in town.

What got you into stage managing?

When I was in high school I started to work on the high school plays. I worked backstage at a local semiprofessional theatre. There wasn't always a lot of money involved, but I was always able to find people who were happy to have me as an apprentice or an intern. In return I got a lot of experience.

So you didn't go to school?

No. I started right out of high school. I've been very, very lucky and haven't really been out of work for about 10 years.

What is your responsibility on the show?

We're responsible for maintaining the artistic integrity of the show. After the show opens, the director leaves. I'm responsible for watching the show, taking any acting or technical notes, passing them on to make sure that what the director intended is still what is happening in the show. We're also responsible for cuing the show.

What do you really like about being a stage manager?

Each day is a new day. If something goes a little wrong one day we have another chance to do it over again the next day.

Is there anything you don't like about being a stage manager?

I don't like that we usually work in a place with no windows. We don't get to see the outdoors much.

What do you see yourself doing in 5 years?

Maybe moving up into management. Maybe producing.

What about travel?

I've been travelling for about 5 years with *Phantom of the Opera, Miss Saigon,* and *Joseph and the Amazing Technicolor Dreamcoat.* You get to see the country, you get to see a lot of different theatres. There are a lot of different challenges: new people, new stage hands, new local conditions.

The First Day in a New Town

It's different on different types of shows. If you are in a "bus and truck" show, you'll come in on the same day, or the day before you have a performance. You and the production carpenter will assess what can or cannot fit into the building, if an advance trip hasn't been done. Then you start to unload the show. The local crew and the road crew will unload the show and put it up. The electricians will put all the lights up. The sound people will put all the sound equipment up. Sometimes on a "bus and truck" the stage manager will help focus the lights: meaning they'll stand on the stage and say "focus the light here on me and make these cuts in the lights." At the same time, again depending on the type of show it is, the orchestra is having an orchestra rehearsal in the lobby or another space. Then about 5 o'clock on the day we have a show that night, the cast will come onto the stage for the first time. They'll walk the crossovers. The stage managers will tell them if there's anything different in the show or if anything's been cut. The wardrobe people will come in and go over all the quick changes, same with the hair people. Then we do the show right at 8 o'clock.

Let's Meet...

Dawn Massaro
Stunt Show Stage Manager

Dawn works hard to make sure all of the explosions in her stunt show go off with just the right bang.

How did you get involved with tech work?

When I was in college I was a fashion major, but I didn't like the sewing classes I had to take. I got into working with the theatre program helping with costumes, and that led me to change my major to drama.

What do you like about technical theatre?

I like so many things about it. So many interesting things are involved with theatre, especially outdoor shows. With the indoor shows you get the lighting and the sound. So many different effects are coming out now. You use fireworks and air cannons.

Is there anything you don't like?

Sure. The hours are very hard. But it all pays off in the end. When you end up with a product you really enjoy and that you're really proud of, the hours are well worth it.

Do you have any special training?

You learn as you go. You pick up things from different jobs you work in, and you use all of those. Anything you've learned, you use running a show. Like with most stage shows, a stage manager is backstage the whole time. I never see the show unless I'm covering for the company manager.

Do you use any special skills?

Over the years I've learned skills. How to load or disable fireworks. I've learned a lot about air cannons and flame units; I didn't know any of that before I started. It depends on how good you want to be. If you want to know what you're doing or just run it. Stage managers in theatre don't know about this stuff, normally, because they don't use it. It's good for me to know, because it's an extra thing under my belt.

What advice do you have?

Assist the technical staff of theatres as much as possible, even if it's for free, because the knowledge you get is well worth it. The younger you start, the easier it is to get work as you get older. The more you learn, the better chances you have of becoming very successful.

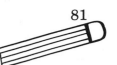

Dawn Sets Up a Stunt Show

When Dawn comes to work, all the vehicles are pulled out. The crew maintains the vehicles, and makes sure everything is connected and everything runs right. After that's done, Dawn supervises the crew to see that everything is set the correct way. Safety is a very, very major factor when a show is presented outdoors. So many things can go wrong.

During the show, Dawn runs backstage. She calls cues to the crew to enable certain pyro (or fireworks) to trigger breakaways. She supervises costume changes and clears vehicles. She watches for any safety hazards on stage. She tries to keep as close an eye as she can from backstage to make sure that when something goes up, there are no residual fires. She communicates with the technical director in the booth. He tells her if something's wrong. He's Dawn's eyes on stage.

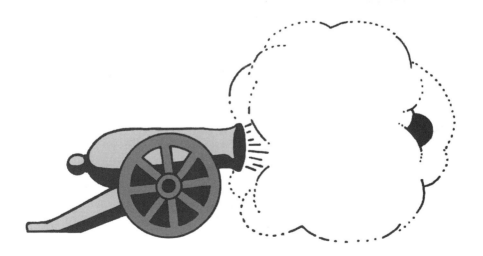

Success Stories

Jennifer Tipton began her career as a lighting designer working for choreographer Paul Taylor. Ms. Tipton's interest in dance has led her to design for a number of famous dancers, including Mikhail Baryshnikov, Robert Joffrey, and choreographer Twyla Tharp. In 1991, she made the step to directing with her production of *The Tempest* at the Guthrie Theatre (Minneapolis).

Adrianne Lobel trained with world-famous set designer Ming Cho Lee and is known for her very daring and creative sets. She has designed sets for several of director Peter Sellars' plays, including 1988's *The Mirage of Figaro,* set in Trump Towers in New York, and the Glyndebourne production of *The Magic Flute,* set in southern California.

Considered one of the most important American set designers of the century, Ming Cho Lee didn't even come to America until he was 19. Born in Shanghai in 1930, Lee has had very little work appear on Broadway. Instead, he chooses to concentrate on productions with the New York Shakespeare Festival and the New York City Opera. Recently, Lee has taken time away from his designing schedule to devote himself more to teaching. He heads the Yale School of Drama's design program.

Find Out More

What It's Like to Work Backstage

Working backstage comes with a lot of expectations. If you become a theatrical technician, you will be asked to:

Work very quietly while a performance is going on.

Take direction.

Work with actors and other technicians.

Put in a lot of time getting ready for the show.

Be there whenever the show is being performed.

Travel wherever the show takes you.

Do a lot of different types of tasks every day.

Ask questions when you don't know what to do.

All of these things contribute to a successful show. If you're involved, there is nothing finer than sharing in the applause.

INDEX